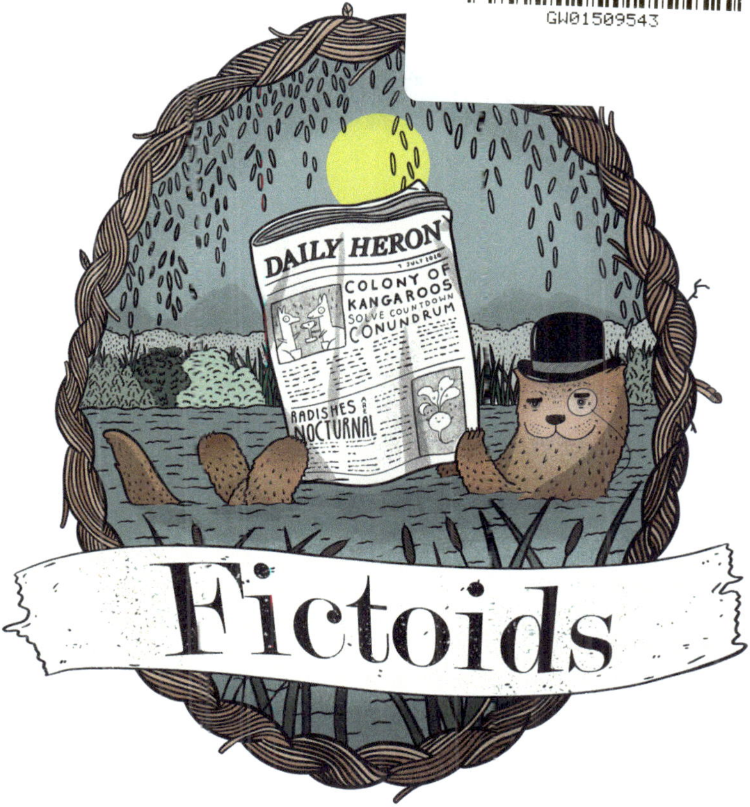

Fictoids

By Pete Hawkins & Andy Kind

About The Publisher

McKnight & Bishop are always on the lookout for new authors and ideas for new books. If you write or if you have an idea for a book, please email: **info@mcknightbishop.com** Some things we love are undiscovered authors, open-source software, Creative Commons, crowd-funding, Amazon/Kindle, social networking, faith, laughter and new ideas.

Visit us at **www.mcknightbishop.com**

Copyright © Pete Hawkins & Andy Kind 2020

The rights of Pete Hawkins & Andy Kind to be identified as the Author s of this Work have been asserted by them in accordance with Section 77 of the Copyright, Designs and Patents Act 1988.

All rights reserved. No part of this book may be reproduced, stored on a retrieval system or transmitted in any form or by any means without prior permission in writing of the publisher nor be otherwise circulated in any form of binding or cover other than that in which it is here published without a similar condition being imposed upon the subsequent publisher.

The views expressed in this work are solely those of the author and do not necessarily reflect the views of the publisher, and the publisher hereby disclaims any responsibility for them.

ISBN 978-1-905691-64-7
A CIP catalogue record for this book is available from the British Library.

Published by McKnight & Bishop Ltd
26 Walworth Crescent, Darlington, DL3 0TX

Printed by United Print, London WC2B 5AH

Thanks to Matt & Ryan (the House of Fun team).
Love to my kids, Amy, Adam & Lucy.
Most of all, my amazing wife Steph.
Love you forever sweetie.

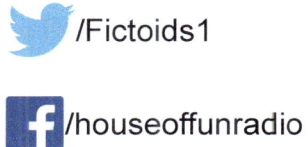 /Fictoids1

/houseoffunradio

P.H.

This book is for Ruth Henson,
who has always smiled at silliness,
no matter what.

 @AndyKindComedy

A.K.

Sven Frankfurter
Paivas, Portugal

♥ 💬

488,015 Likes

Otters are flammable.

#Tarkathehotter #organickindling

Olga Brkić
Hemelveerdegem, Belgium

♥ 💬

932,013 Likes

Female earth worms taste of pomegranate, whilst male ones have no distinguishable taste.

#5aday #yumyum

Timur Kryukov
Haugesund, Norway

♥ 💬

750,777 Likes

Badgers levitate when no one is looking.

#badgermagic #floatywildlife

Ngọt Trương
Whyalla Stuart, Australia

♥ 💬

104,541 Likes

Cocker Spaniels are the only breed of dog that can wink.

#flirtypup #winkingwoofer

Kyle Simpson
Molins de Rei, Spain

208,173 Likes

Parsnips can change gender when threatened.

#vegetabledefense #neverhitalady

 Radosława Zielinska
Rock Rapids, United States

324,815 Likes

Manx cats are allergic to Maltesers.

#chocandchoke #givethematoblerone

 Logan Armstrong
Łódź, Poland

504,245 Likes

Marmosets are 23% made of potassium.

#healthyalternative #77percentevil

 Bastian Lundqvist
Velké Hosterádky, Czech Republic

373,767 Likes

Modern cats have 11 lives, rather than the 9 their predecessors enjoyed. This is down to improvements in veterinary health care, and also inflation.

#livinglonger #catsocialcare

Karen Schmidt
Barneveld, Netherlands

320,717 Likes

Red Squirrels are just Grey Squirrels with a tan.

#DavidDickinson #Essexwildlife

Sointu Jyrkiäinen
Chicago, United States

254,706 Likes

Leave a language tape playing overnight and your gerbil can learn to speak Portuguese.

#bilingualrodent #talentedpets

Emiliano Ferri
Malton, Canada

462,908 Likes

Pineapples believe in original sin.

#naughtyfruit #guiltypleasure

Elle Lurd
Seaview, New Zealand

774,238 Likes

Pelicans see Dutch people in black and white only.

#monchromeseabirds
#colourabovesealevel

Spencer Simpson
Rubí, Spain

574,015 Likes

To avoid hurting their feelings, Bald Eagles must now be referred to as "Follicly Challenged Eagles".

#sensativebirdsofprey #combover

 Andreas Kristiansen
Castro Marim, Portugal

577,025 Likes

If you lay the intestines of a fully-grown African Rhino in a straight line across a school classroom, the children will have to be sent home and the teacher sacked and imprisoned.

#scienceinaction #safarisogood

 Mee Cheng
Sievi, Finland

12,610 Likes

Lemmings experience time in reverse. So, to them, they are jumping out of the sea and onto tall cliffs.

#jumpingtotheirlives #goingupintheworld

 Haddad Najjar
Potgieterus, South Africa

130,148 Likes

It takes the humble Anteater over 43 years to produce enough saliva to spit just once.

#gobbyanimal #savethephlegm

Chukwumaobim Onwubiko
København K, Denmark

473,769 Likes

Laboratory tests have proven that stinging nettles will not grow when Madonna's greatest hits Volume 1 is played to them on a continuous loop. And frankly, why would they?

#papadontsting #materialplant

 ترلان صادق زاده
Elvas, Portugal

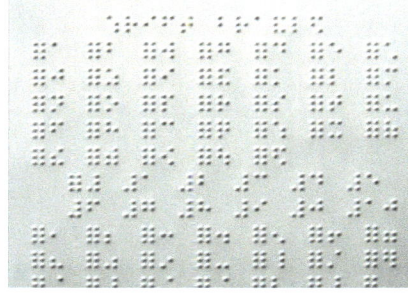

385,995 Likes

To improve Zoo safety, from early 2020 all animals will have their species names embossed on them in braille. This will help blind people in the event of the animal escaping.

#touchysubject #healthandsafetygonemad

 Zumorito
Zaldibar, Spain

224,747 Likes

Tests have proven that the humble Guinea Pig is not so humble at all. In fact, it is the most egotistical of all house pets.

#fullofitsself #toobigforitscage

 Carlos Sousa
Duque de Caxias, Brazil

491,078 Likes

Hedgehogs can see wi-fi.

#broadbandwildlife #techsavvyanimals

Emma Buckmaster
Crymelon, Australia

139,393 Likes

A West African Wildebeest has just been twinned with Tewksbury.

#separatedatbirth #localgnus

 Jarmila Bajerová
Katowice, Poland

929,822 Likes

If they are unable to hear each other, budgerigars have been known to communicate using semaphore.

#flaggingbadly #learntotweet

 Rana Nessarc
Cox, Spain

945,425 Likes

Koi Carp are not as coy as the name suggests. In fact, they have been known to brazenly slap fishermen.

#schoolviolence #fishslappingdance

 安沛 鄧
Goiânia, Brazil

383,548 Likes

Because of efforts to open top jobs to minority groups, the new CEO of British Gas is a 7-foot long Conger eel.

#inclusivityworks #eeldowell

Vanja Debeljak
Riby, United Kingdom

493,318 Likes

A colony of kangaroos at Colchester Zoo have been trained to solve the Countdown Conundrum.

#aconsenantpleaseCarol #hopoit

Nanna Dahl
Grgar, Slovenia

646,924 Likes

Badgers do not believe in the existence of Swindon and can become quite passive-aggressive if you try to raise the issue in conversation.

#leaveitKeith #youstartingsomething

Kobor Horon
Mariscala, Uruguay

882,388 Likes

Shaving an otter produces enough fur to cover another bald otter of the same size.

#makessensewhenyouthinkaboutit
#noaftershaveplease

Gilly Grubb
Jaboatão dos Guararapes, Brazil

375,108 Likes

London Zoo has the UK's first wi-fi enabled Red Panda, after a successful attempt to cross-breed an adult male with a BT Home Hub.

#onlineexhibits #pandahotspot

Nicki Dröge
Peckforton, United Kingdom

449,715 Likes

If you rub a fully-grown Egyptian Mongoose against a shower curtain, it produces enough static electricity to light a 20W bulb for 4½ minutes.

#scienceisgreat #bannedfromhomebase

Helga Kubišová
Älandsbro, Sweden

449,041 Likes

Zebras prefer the term 'Mixed Heritage Horses'.

#youcantsaythat #hurtfeelings

Emil Salcido
Temvria, Cyprus

436,330 Likes

Cats have such acute vision that they can see a film before it's been made.

#nospoliers #catpremiere

Eva Hill
Bridgeville, United States

71,195 Likes

You can lead a horse chestnut to water and it'll probably have a drink.

#alcoholictrees #rootoftheproblem

Nebay Mehari
Danmarkshavn, Green and

309,274 Likes
All Giraffes are Hindu.
#headintheclouds #sanskritsafaris

Valdemar Longhole
Milton BC, Australia

610,888 Likes
Police dogs who jump through flaming hoops are actually badly burned and are assassinated shortly after.
#cruelbuttrue #hotdogs

Kazuyoshi Onodera
Trois Rivieres, Canada

469,603 Likes
The Farthing Wood fox now works with ex-offenders.
#secondcareer #communitysupportfox

Maddalena Lettiere
Tromsø, Norway

596,781 Likes
Radishes are nocturnal.
#vegetablesofthenight #2amsalad

Jonas Holst
Majšperk, Slovenia

350,400 Likes

Pumas don't really exist. They are just in your mind.

#allacon #fakecatnews

Lechi Akhtakhanov
São Gonçalo, Brazil

964,930 Likes

Flea is the longest word in the English language - it just hides it well.

#foldsupsmall #lotsofsilentletters

Sophie Faubert
Campinas, Brazil

634,251 Likes

In 1923, there was a massive Christian revival amongst foxes. 40% of woodland creatures at the time professed an active faith in Christ. Owing to poor discipleship, that figure is now closer to 7%.

#praisehimbygoingthroughthebins #cunningsaviour

Barbra Adamlje
St. Jakob, Austria

58,224 Likes

Contrary to popular science, there is in fact a small group of Dutch Elm trees left in England. They wander from place to place, living a nomadic lifestyle and telling sad stories.

#gypsytrees #havediseasewilltravel

Ane Larsen
Ringsted, Denmark

509,900 Likes

Nobody has ever found a second satisfactory way to skin a cat.

#keeptrying #thetruthisoutthere

Lete Girma
Hämeenlinna, Finland

415,577 Likes

Astronomer Russell Grant used to play Rugby League for Widnes

#alwaysgame #worthatry

Kyo Vloedgraven
London, Canada

92,353 Likes

Ipswich Town won the 1978 FA Cup Final via the Duckworth/Lewis method.

#breakthedeadlock #footballhistory

Kerimsolta Melikov
Tammevaldma, Estonia

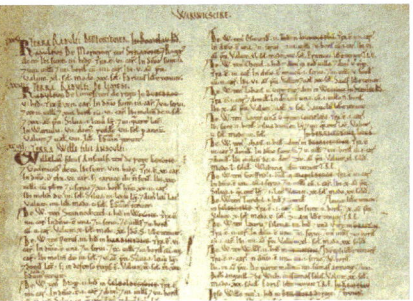

389,822 Likes

The first recorded mentioning of Plymouth Argyle Football Club is in the Domesday Book of 1086.

#olderthannottscounty #yeoldepilgrims

Katrine Andersen
Zwaag, Netherlands

179,984 Likes

The temperature of Tottenham Hotspur has actually dropped by 1.8 degrees Celsius since they last won the First Division in 1961.

#coldstreak #chillyLondon

Line Jørgensen
Hamilton, Canada

101,762 Likes

In 2024, Swingball becomes an official Olympic sport.

#retrosports #Britishbulldognext

Trine Hedegaard
Åsbro, Sweden

371,127 Likes

Racing Commentator Jon McCririck's hats are visible from the International Space Station.

#bighead #whowantstobeamilliner

Markku Jutila
Dominguiso, Portugal

90,332 Likes

The Dalai Lama is a lifelong supporter of Scottish Football Team, Hamilton Academicals. He even invented his own chant: 'Score another goal, Hamilton Academicals' he will often sing, to the tune of Sussudio by Phil Collins.

#likesahalftimepie #Buddhawouldacoulda

Orlagh Duncan
Žamberk, Czech Republic

552,961 Likes

From next year, Darts players can use a "Joker" to double the score of any 3-dart combination.

#itsaknockout #getthecalculatorout

Ladislav Čada
Toronto, Canada

346,664 Likes

The stripes in the grass of Wimbledon's centre court are caused by electrical disturbances from the District Line, which runs directly underneath.

#undergroundoverground #earthfault

Yobachi Onwuamaeze
Luulupe, Estonia

669,133 Likes

On the west side of the UK, an area the size of Wales is known as 'Wales'.

#referencepoint #itfits

J'Gira Grendle
Macon, Belgium

248,223 Likes

Oswestry Town FC are an English football club who play in a Welsh league. They are the only team in the UK where the players' names on the shirts appear in two languages.

#bilingual #thereslovely

George Sundström
Liten, Czech Republic

80,943 Likes

Olympic equestrian rider, William Fox-Pitt, is the first person in the UK to have a sawn-off double-barrelled surname

#posh&armed #historicname

Vaka Björnsdóttir
Λευκωσια, Cyprus

571,124 Likes

Rugby derives from the saxon word rågbar - meaning 'not as good as football'.

#eggball #notgoodenoughatkicking

Radek Pokorný
Danmarkshavn, Greenland

620,374 Likes

The original badge for the England football team, before the introduction of the 3 Lions, featured a packet of Salt and Vinegar Crisps.

#Walkers #barsnacks

Feliks Jasiński
Dion, Belgium

47,546 Likes

The Scottish game of Shinty is sexually aggressive towards other sports.

#predatory #alphamalesport

Ćazim Bajič
Bonneville, Belgium

764,091 Likes

Theo Walcott entered Britain's Got Talent as a footballer and didn't make the live shows.

#toughatthetop #nofromme

کامران داوودی
Durazno, Uruguay

353,762 Likes

Former Arsenal Manager, Arsène Wenger, carried a spiked mace inside his long coat to punish players who under-performed.

#toughlove #isthatamaceinyourpocket

Kristian Knudsen
Hector, United States

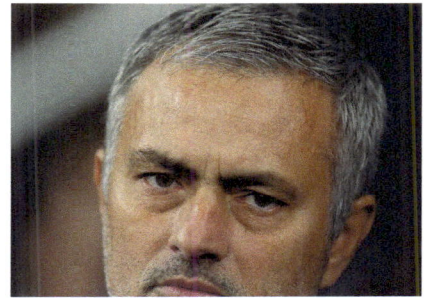

72,213 Likes

José Mourinho forces his teams to listen to the entire Lord of the Rings score on match days. Anyone who flinches is immediately transfer-listed.

#classicalmanagement #donttwitch

Livia Martins
Glamsbjerg, Denmark

882,858 Likes

There is a working snake pit under Twickenham.

#takingthehiss #whydidithavetobesnakes

Gyuszi Szôlôsi
Suwałki, Poland

875,994 Likes

Before Euro 2012, the FA were considering swapping the national anthem for Ding Dong the Witch is Dead. They were dissuaded by a well-oiled petition campaign led by John Fashanu.

#singalongWembley #Fashthebash

Einara Ragnarsdóttir
Mansfield Park, Australia

418,238 Likes

The England Cricket team have a secret ritual. Before the first innings, former "On Safari" host and pantomime heart-throb Christopher Biggins runs into the dressing room totally nude and is chased with towels. The team have never lost when this has taken place.

#wobblybits #takehisbailsoff

 Nwachinemelu Nkemakonam
Fülöpháza, Hungary

773,907 Likes

Due to a miscommunication, Mo Farah's CBE was awarded to him by Honor Blackman.

#unfortuatetypo #jogonpal

 Rinkashifu
Stanger, South Africa

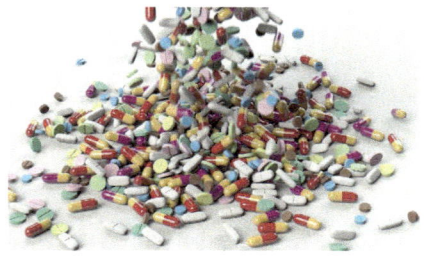

859,594 Likes

The Cold War was actually won by Blackburn Rovers, but they were later stripped of the title after a drugs scandal.

#nottobesniffedat #classAteam

 Matheus Lima
Samambaia, Brazil

177,349 Likes

Lewis Hamilton is a wi-fi hotspot.

#fastbroadband #theinternetscrashed

由美子 山県
Louis Trichardt, South Africa

5,060 Likes

36% of Guernsey is below eye level.

#Channeleyelands #sinkingfeeling

 **Michal Kubík**
Strovolos, Cyprus

782,867 Likes

The average British man is Geoff Williams from Solihull.

#lovegeoff #stuckinthemiddlewithGeoff

 Stefán Hjálmtýsson
Vantaa, Finland

661,463 Likes

In 1874, the most recorded crime in the Isle of Wight was 'pretending to be a ghost'.

#woo #caughtbytheghoulies

 Trai Võ
Bromley, New Zealand

264,705 Likes

In the Winter Olympics, Speed Skating has proved vastly more popular than Heroin Bobsleigh or Marijuana Ski Jumping.

#classasport #pointlessdrugtests

Kimiho Ooyama
Dax, France

591,298 Likes

Carlisle used to be in Essex but was given to Cumbria after Pitt the Younger lost a poker game in 1594.

#allin #luckofthecards

 Martim Pereira
Fáskrúðsfjörður, Iceland

816,124 Likes

In 1978, excessive breeding led to the UK's first Ford Cortina cull. The population was reduced by two-thirds in just 7 months. Occasional sightings of the Cortina are still recorded in Cornwall and northerly parts of Scotland.

#rarecars #populationcontrol

 ทวีสิทธิ์ บุญมา
Erfurt, Germany

48,035 Likes

In 1962, Easter fell earlier than any other year in the entire century. New Year's Day was in August, Halloween slipped back to May and St George's Day was celebrated on alternate Tuesdays.

#diarymixup #changeisasgoodasarest

 Mette Jakobsen
Goiânia, Brazil

719,971 Likes

The cost of London housing reached a new high last week when a single portion Cottage Pie was sold in Kensington for £472,000.

#howmuch #claimonexpenses

Hannah Holland
Saint-Laurent-du-Var, France

922,370 Likes

Owing to the impact of climate change, Cheddar Gorge in the Mendip Hills is now classified as extra mature.

#planetunderthreat #crackinghillsGromit

 Gaweł Kucharski
Postmasburg, South Africa

894,955 Likes

In order to boost numbers, London Zoo is to start a breeding program for Rag and Bone men.

#youdirtyoldman #Steptoeridesagain

 Marco Boehm
Pinhal Novo, Portugal

865,298 Likes

History scholars at Oxford University have proven that the year 1973 was completely fictional.

#neverhappened #allinthemind

 Brigitte Theissen
El Paso, Spain

687,197 Likes

Most illegal migrants to the UK claim their reason for coming here is to watch old episodes of "Homes under the Hammer".

#onlyinEngland #daytimetelly

Hussein Eliasson
Mosfellsbær, Iceland

407,688 Likes

A Primary School in Durham is lifting its ban on children bringing harpoon guns into the classroom. 'About time, too,' said Billy Whelk, aged 5.

#notinWales #whoneedsnerfguns

Antu Pina
Berente, Hungary

52,875 Likes

Scarfell Pike is to be lowered by 350m to improve wheelchair access. The removed soil will be used to build a new hill named Scarface Plank.

#cateringforall #wheeliegoodidea

Dino Sanabria
Raahe, Finland

845,502 Likes

Lloyds Of London has sold its 19% stake in Ricky Martin.

#livinglavidasoldhim #equityrelease

Giỏi Chu
Netzschkau, Germany

229,239 Likes

The London Mint is so called because all British coins used to have a hole in the middle and/or were chewy.

#richsnacks #freshmoney

Iheatu Dilibe
Tzaneen, South Africa

993,018 Likes

Do you know how the River Thames got its name? Because it's full of water, making it a river.

#soobvious #makessense

Eupraxia Zubareva
Sommerhausen, Germany

871,813 Likes

The most popular High Street name in the UK is 'High Street'.

#duh #figureitout

Numa Samaniego
ΜελανΔΡα, Cyprus

972,597 Likes

Wally has finally been found. He was in the middle aisle of a Lincolnshire Aldi, buying a fishing rod.

#myturntohide #gonefishing

Tiffany Miser
Montpellier, France

784,532 Likes

Due to the magnetic pull of the Norwegian Coastline, the city of York has moved 12.4m east over the last 9 years. York denies all knowledge and gets anxious if you try to raise it in conversation.

#donttellhimPike #vikingsatheart

Mediha Štakolič
Olsztyn, Poland

839,167 Likes

Skegness is the only town in the UK which can be navigated to using only one's sense of smell.

#nottobesniffedat #whiffy

健太 板山
Bresternica, Slovenia

111,518 Likes

The village of Thorney has been twinned with Tom Cruise.

#missionpossible #biggerthanhim

Karen Hauksdóttir
København V, Denmark

798,417 Likes

83% of all the UK's Garlic Naan Breads are consumed in Lowestoft.

#lovecurry #localdelicacy

Milanja Radež
Rýmarov, Czech Republic

848,780 Likes

The Thames Flood barrier is a mirage.

#notreallythere #trickofthelight

 桐子 飯干
Tänikon, Switzerland

760,447 Likes

On average, 1 in 3 UK households have an unopened packet of Eat Me dates at any given time.

#yuck #noonelikesthem

 Marcella Fiorentino
Svaneke, Denmark

877,789 Likes

In the UK, starlings are outnumbered by scrabble tiles by a ratio of 27 to 1.

#theyreeverywhere #triplewordflock

 Chidalu Chidozie
Beaverton, United States

7,580 Likes

In Birmingham, you are never more than 12 feet from a plastic teaspoon.

#theygeteverywhere #usefulforabrew

 Lando Buijs
Zastávka u Brna, Czech Republic

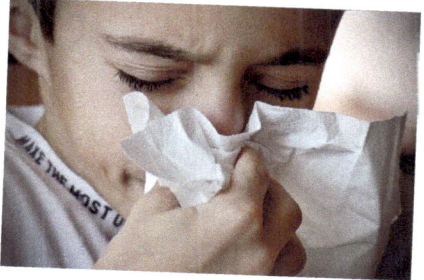

621,468 Likes

The town of Margate in Kent is allergic to flowers.

#sniffles #blessyou

Aliisa Helkovaara
Höfn, Iceland

590,295 Likes

From next April, a Catholic church in Kidderminster is opening the UK's first communion drive through.

#golarge #canIhavefrieswiththat

 Erik Mathiassen
Laksevåg, Norway

41,990 Likes

A Welsh energy firm has become the first in the world to generate electricity by harnessing the power of drizzle. This means, from next year, Llandudno will be self-sufficient in electricity production.

#genius #alwaysraining

 Maria Strand
Kalo Chorio Lafkas, Cyprus

582,413 Likes

The conjoined cities of Brighton and Hove have been separated after a mammoth 24-year operation. Hove keeps the night buses whilst Brighton gets the recycling collected every alternate Tuesday.

#messydivorce #mumneverlikedyou

 Elina Sokolova
Bairro da Costa, Portugal

250,158 Likes

The River Thames was dug in November 1939 as a moat in case of German Invasion. In the event of an assault, all bridges were to be destroyed except Tower Bridge, which would be raised and could only be lowered when the correct password was shouted across the river.

#defenseoftherealm #dontlikeitupem

Арсений Уваров
Ikerasassuaq, Greenland

157,082 Likes

Nigel Willis from Oswestry has just smashed the world record for being on hold on a telephone. He has been listening to his energy company playing 'Green Sleeves' on a continuous loop for 23 days and 4 hours.

#takingages #press1forhelp

 Арсений Уваров
Hubberg, Austria

629,752 Likes

The growing tensions between North and South-ampton have grown to such an extent that Northampton has recently filed for divorce. Southampton is said to be 'sad but a bit relieved to be honest.'

#onthecards #Imkeepingthecdcollection

 Людмила Андреева
Le Cannet, France

593,681 Likes

There used to be another major city between Glasgow and Edinburgh. However, in the early 1940s it was found guilty of feeding national secrets to the Nazis, and was shot as a spy.

#roughjustice #erasedfromhistory

 Magðalena Marinósdóttir
Ash Magna, United Kingdom

633,336 Likes

In some parts of Wiltshire, Golden Syrup is considered an aphrodisiac.

#helloladies #getlucky

大地 釜
Brastad, Sweden

156,228 Likes

From next year, the Governments OFSTED inspectors will start assessing schools of fish in British Territorial waters.

#oceansofwork #raisingstandards

 Panteleimon Alekseyeva
Kielce, Poland

805,322 Likes

To allow for falling rates of numeracy in the UK, the Metro Newspaper is to start running a binary bingo game, only using the numbers 0 & 1.

#fordummies #evengrannycanplay

 بختیار حکمت
Simala, Italy

193,784 Likes

A new series of flood defences has been built around a factory in Carlisle. The factory produces 93% of the UK's stock of water biscuits.

#crackers #protectthevaluables

 Páley Indriðadóttir
Rudolfov, Czech Republic

470,552 Likes

The road network in Milton Keynes is arranged to assist lost drivers. If you turn right at every roundabout you come to, you eventually arrive at the town's main railway station.

#handy #whoneedsasatnav

Madihah Tannous
Okotoks, Canada

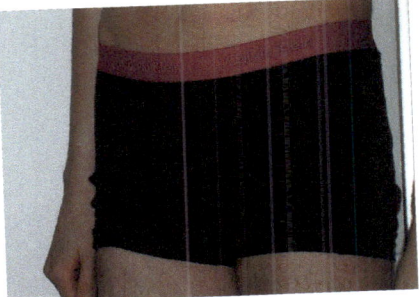

342,088 Likes

Due to the amount of underwear hanging on British washing lines at any given time, Calvin Klein have started receiving royalties from Google Street View.

#productplacement #itsallpants

Markku Rehn
Vagos, Portugal

746,871 Likes

In some parts of rural Wiltshire, witch doctors used lottery scratch cards to predict the future.

#ancienttraditions #itcouldbeyou

Iveta Spurná
Peristeronari, Cyprus

724,543 Likes

The densest substance known to man is London's Hard Rock Café, measuring in at 75,000kg per cubic centimetre.

#heavyman #geology&burgers

Otutodilinna Izuchukwu
Balclutha, New Zealand

809,518 Likes

In 2015, there were record sales in the Newcastle Apple store on the launch day of their new "Why I-phone 6".

#newphonepet #Shearer

# Božidar Klarić
Porto Alegre, Brazil

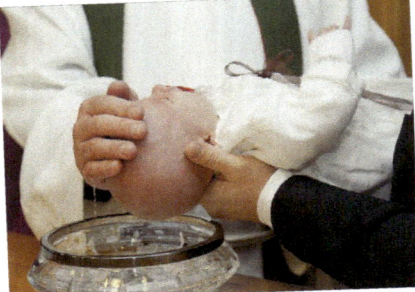

573,560 Likes

No-one is the UK has been christened Roland since the appearance of the character of the same name in Grange Hill. Experts predict, if this decline is not reversed, the name will become extinct upon the death of comedian Rowland Rivron.

#dyingout #reversethetrend

# Iole Cardona
Fene, Spain

362,279 Likes

It is now believed that the counters in branches of Greggs emit a low-level gravitational pull. This explains why obese people are pulled into the shop - not by a lack of willpower or the desire for a lukewarm pasty, but by a simple application of Newtonian Science.

#cantfightit #irresistable

Fadi Daher
Burradoo, Australia

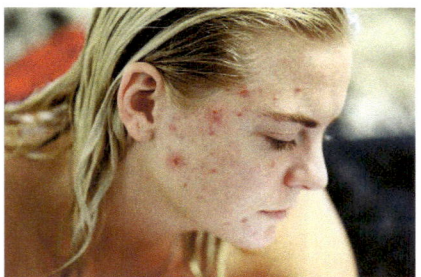

631,986 Likes

A teenager from Grimsby, who suffers from chronic acne, has sprouted a braille version of the complete works of Shakespeare on her chin.

#spotthebard #isthisazitiseebeforeme

Arvid Lindqvist
Utrera, Spain

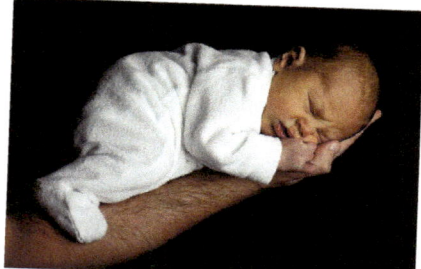

811,750 Likes

All residents of Andover are born bilingual. However, tests have shown that the second language is normally forgotten by the time they are 4 months old.

#losetheknack #younglearners

遥 長久
Rock Creek, Canada

48,285 Likes

A London rental firm is now offering timeshare parking spaces in some of the capital's busiest streets. A 4-hour stay once a year, in a marked bay on Regent Street, will set you back £825.

#onlyfortherich #getabusinstead

K'Kehla Daa'maq
Kal nad Kanalom, Slovenia

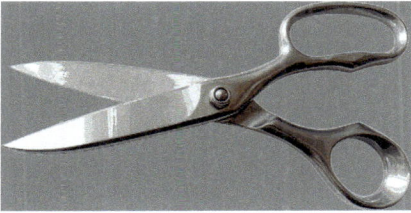

326,034 Likes

Health experts in Scotland have warned that there is a 1 in 3 chance of children suffering an injury if they run whilst playing a game of rock, paper, scissors.

#dontdoit #youllhaveyoureyeout

Krystyn Król
Alice, South Africa

833,392 Likes

After checking against a Dulux colour chart, the Isle of Wight will now be known as the Isle of Beige.

#touchupthepaintwork #faded

Emile Jessen
Spjald, Denmark

889,376 Likes

To improve the climate in the North of England, approval has been given to the construction of a 400ft high patio heater on the moors above Huddersfield.

#globalwarming #thinkoutsidethebox

一樹 下司
Paris, France

879,660 Likes

To reflect the changing attitudes to gun crime in the UK, Aldershot will be renamed Aldertazered.

#selfdefense #disablethecriminals

 Mahbubah Issa
Drammen, Norway

799,103 Likes

Just 3 miles south of the Scottish border, archaeologists have discovered evidence of a Roman convenience store. This is being dubbed as "Hadrian's Walmart".

#lovehistory #everylittlehelps

 令宜 袁
Sant Andreu de la Barca, Spain

950,144 Likes

Due to an error on the ballot paper, an earth worm was elected Mayor of Halifax in 2005. He successfully stood for re-election 3 years later.

#doingagreatjob #betterthanBoris

 Marcela Hradilová
Reykjavík, Iceland

601,842 Likes

There are no Butcher's shops in the whole of Wessex.

#oddity #vegancounty

Amelia Lorenzo
Sertã, Portugal

981,497 Likes

The London Eye will be closed next year for a cataract operation.

#showingitsage #simpleprocedure

Công Vương
Rüti bei Riggisberg, Switzerland

963,143 Likes

Due to an oversight, the City of Winchester was not shown on any Ordinance Survey map until 1996.

#nevermisseditanyway #hiddeninplainsight

Nora Björklund
Aglientu, Italy

387,627 Likes

The London Borough of Croydon is attempting to power its streetlights by harnessing the power of negativity. This came after one of their technicians had a "light bulb" moment that he thought would never work.

#whatsthepoint #boundtofail

Dexter Lachapelle
Elizabeth City, United States

616,385 Likes

The British Government has announced that the losers of the next two national referendums will go against each other in a dance off.

#voteforthefoxtrot #moveslikeJagger

Noël Gamelin
Tuahiwi, New Zealand

886,209 Likes

Medway district council has ordered the UK's first ever Chav Cull. They are proposing that up to 85% of teenagers wearing Burberry clothing and listening to Grime music will be humanely destroyed.

#claimbackthestreets #thintheherd

Зоя Самойлова
Hrísey, Iceland

720,653 Likes

The national flower of the Isle of Skye is self-raising.

#inbread #localtraditions

Kate Hicks
Stonewall, Canada

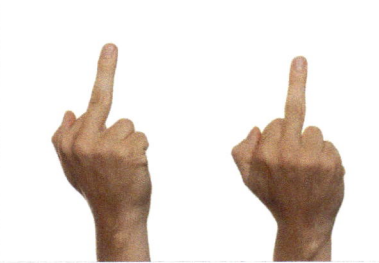

230,141 Likes

The British Sign Language alphabet has 27 letters. There is an extra one between R and S after the person dictating them for the first time twitched at the wrong moment.

#gettheshakes #spellingbee

Autumn Wallace
Parque Carrasco, Uruguay

885,596 Likes

In the Orkney Islands in 1951, the first wind turbine was connected to the National Grid. Unfortunately, the wiring was back to front and the turbine drew electricity from the supply and turned it into wind by mistake.

#oops #breezy

Szescx Gere
Λευκωσια, Cyprus

586,162 Likes

Inspired by David Blaine's plexiglass box stunt, two salesmen from Milton Keynes were suspended above the town's Railway Station in a glass squash court. They intended to play continuously for 3 weeks but stopped after just 28 minutes, when the ball fell out of the box through a small air hole.

#canIhavemyballback #takeiteasylads

Claire Picard
Kirchstetten, Austria

207,605 Likes

It took the Bristol Women's Institute 17 months to knit the replacement chains for the Clifton Suspension Bridge.

#sistersaredoingit #knitonepearlone

Birk Karlsson
Sayada Nord, Tunisia

688,496 Likes

To provide metal for the war effort, the Blackpool Tower was demolished in 1940 and replaced with an identical one made from Plasticine.

#doingtheirbit #giveJerryabloodynose

Marija Andreja Krsteva
Casino La Goulette, Tunisia

260,219 Likes

At Lizard Point in Cornwall the tide does not go in or out; rather it remains constant. To overcome this the National Trust has installed hydraulic rams under the beach to raise and lower it, producing a simulated tidal effect.

#genius #naturefindsaway

Cupido Bianchi
Warrachie, Australia

243,821 Likes

Copies of the 1986 Yellow Pages for the Wakefield area now fetch up to £3000 each on the black market.

#illicitpurchase #wannabuyaphonebook

Sally Nyman
Otipua Creek, New Zealand

177,383 Likes

The South Downs in Sussex were built in 1940 as speed bumps, to slow down any potential German Invasion.

#keepthematbay #digforvictory

Mislava Knežević
Vinica, Slovenia

390,444 Likes

From 2022, the Pembrokeshire Coast path in Wales will be the first national trail with an overtaking lane for faster walkers.

#outofmyway #bumblingalong

Kerr Mackenzie
Oleiros, Portugal

683,129 Likes

Peterborough's Queensgate Centre bus station is to be fully enclosed to keep passengers dry. Vehicles will enter through the solid walls via a series of "bus flaps".

#outoftheelements #warm&cozy

Michaela Málková
Kielce, Poland

169,818 Likes

Until the age of 9, native Liverpudlians are only audible to dogs.

#calmdown #talktotheanimals

 Dahlak Yemane
Croxdale, United Kingdom

524,157 Likes

Recent tests by the Environment Agency have proven that the River Nene is now 64% old shopping trolleys.

#fishfo-pounds #risingwaterlevels

 Fiorello Piazza
Finnbogastaðir, Iceland

106,052 Likes

At an archaeological dig in Hereford, remains of the world's first ever limerick were found. Ironically, the discovery was made by a young man from Nantucket, who was digging out stones with a bucket.

#historicalhysterical #hiddengems

 Eden Foley
Terroso, Portugal

171,700 Likes

By law, all shops on Park Lane or Mayfair must accept payment by Monopoly money.

#dontpassgo #getoutofjailfree

سوزان نافه چی
Duncan, Canada

46,834 Likes

Post Office branches in Greater London will become carbon neutral from next year after the installation of new equipment that harnesses the power of grumbling in queues.

#whatsthepoint #beenwaitingages

 Celestyna Jasińska
Chaves, Portugal

319,430 Likes

A team of explorers from Plymouth University are aiming to be the first people to walk, unaided, to the West Pole. It is believed to be located somewhere outside Shrewsbury.

#itsouttheresomewhere
#breakingnewground

 Orazio De Luca
Białystok, Poland

926,650 Likes

Cambridge University has fitted the UK's first "Average IQ" cameras. These measure the mental faculty of visitors, facilitating the quick removal from the campus of any working class people.

#thicko #getoffmyland

 Toàn Dương
København V, Denmark

694,496 Likes

The word Manchester derives from 2 olde Saxon words: 'Manch' meaning 'less pretentious' and 'ester' meaning 'than London'.

#keepitreal #bloodysoutherners

สุศิราธร นามโคตร
Igavere, Estonia

450,182 Likes

The Royal National Lifeboat Institution will have to stop using the acronym RNLI. This is after a successful lawsuit brought by the Reading & Newbury Librarians Incorporated.

#lawsuit #wesawitfirst

 สุศิริทิพย์ อยู่ปราโมทย์
Απεσια, Cyprus

979,384 Likes

To avoid the risks of epilepsy, the Royal Navy are taking special measures with their Morse Code lamps. All messages will be preceded by a warning: "the following message contains flashing images".

#safetyfirst #thatdoesntwork

 Jakob Frydenberg
Jaureguiberry, Uruguay

66,854 Likes

After 11pm in a residential area, it is illegal to use a shoe-horn.

#upsettheneighbours #keepitdown

 ทวีศิลป์ พูนสี
Umeå, Sweden

888,110 Likes

Rutland is the only UK county which refuses to change its clocks to British Summer Time. People leaving the county must wait at the border for one hour, prior to crossing.

#independantliving #setyourwatches

 **Mario Crnić**
Cite Bit Mekka, Tunisia

682,330 Likes

Because it contains pips, the Greenwich Time Signal has been reclassified as a fruit.

#neverknewthat #5aday

 Teresa Abramova
Invercargill Central, New Zealand

702,909 Likes

From next October, the speaking clock is to be fitted with subtitles.

#helpful #whatevernext

 Danuta Kucharska
Givisiez, Switzerland

462,689 Likes

Rotherham is a member of the pulse family.

#reclassification #regularfolk

 Mieszko Olszewski
Vísky u Letovic, Czech Republic

378,164 Likes

When asked what job she would have done had she chosen not to go down the whole Queen path, Elizabeth the Second was quoted as saying 'croupier'.

#wannabet #pokerface

Самира Назарова
Kökar, Finland

413,978 Likes

To raise funds, the Metropolitan Police is to start selling branded board games. The first of these is "Trivial High-Speed Pursuit", where you can stop another player from winning by deploying a stinger.

#slowthemdown #isthisyourquestionsir

Xinh Ngô
Tršice, Czech Republic

905,645 Likes

The BNP aren't racist. The correct term is pigmentally challenged.

#inoffensive #youcantsaythat

'A'ishah Kouri
Toronto, Canada

970,590 Likes

Henry VIII's excuse for having so many wives was that, after a while, he'd learned all of their chess moves off by heart, making 'games night' tedious and predictable.

#freshenitup #7yearitch

Roxanne Hill
Berzona, Switzerland

702,883 Likes

Oliver Cromwell was a successful sitcom writer before he became a puritan.

#gagsterforhire #theoriginalBlackadder

Niklas Kojonkoski
Moravský Krumlov, Czech Republic

463,790 Likes

The War of the Roses went to extra time and penalties.

#settlethescore #replayatWembley

Johnson de Langen
Rotterdam, Netherlands

763,437 Likes

Mime artists are a protected species in Namibia. They are highly prized by poachers for their white gloves.

#glasscaseofemotion
#itsamimefieldouththere

Ajdin Hermansson
Hillsborough, New Zealand

580,434 Likes

The mainstay of the Estonian economy is blancmange farming.

#betterthanjelly #eatwhite

Aimee Hunter
Dover, United States

819,143 Likes

Danish passports are made of Lego.

#thosecrazyDanes #vikingisaverb

Dževahira Semečnik
Haffouz, Tunisia

90,157 Likes

When provoked, all Belgians are adept at juggling.

#youcouldntmakeitup #butwedid

Andrew Aksakov
Trois Rivieres, Canada

916,789 Likes

Betamax video tapes are highly prized in Morocco because they are believed to have mystical powers.

#spooky #quitlivinginthepast

 Juan Chin
Geierschlag, Austria

902,851 Likes

In some parts of Mexico, the turnip is still accepted as legal tender.

#turnipforthebooks #Illpaybycard

 Martha Medhane
Alavus, Finland

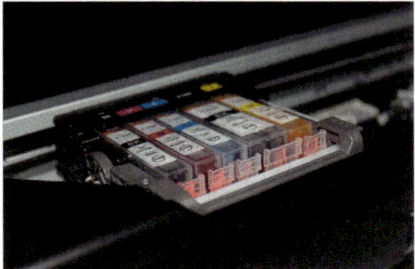

363,431 Likes

A Hewlett Packard printer was sent into geostationary orbit by Russia in 1994 as scientists wanted to see what effect zero gravity would have on Cyan cartridges.

#Iflippinglovescience
#GravitystarringSandraBullock

 Лина Прохорова
Dobova, Slovenia

955,942 Likes

It is said that "Too many cooks spoil the broth". Until recently, no one was sure exactly how many were too many. Scientists at the University of Texas have now proven that the number not to be exceeded is 17.

#ifyoucantstandtheheat #nobodylikessoup

 จิณณวัตร์ นามมหา
Rotterdam, Netherlands

690,704 Likes

The literal translation of San Marino is "nicer than Hemel Hempstead".

#WorldCupminnows
#ateammadeupofpostmen

 Lučko Džeba
Blenheim Central, New Zealand

680,546 Likes

Pencil Sharpeners are considered blasphemous in parts of Bhutan.

#OMGosh #theHisslent

 Iskander Golovanov
Britannia Heights, New Zealand

362,526 Likes

Macclesfield is actually found in the northern part of Mongolia. It just hangs out in Cheshire loads.

#travelboytravel #Genghiscantmorelike

 Oliver Østergaard
Neplachovce, Czech Republic

433,173 Likes

A Swedish tourist, who went missing in Croydon 14 years ago, has been found safe and well in the bedding department of the local Ikea. He didn't know the English for "Way Out".

#stoppedformeatballs #probablycalledLars

Tomáš Kořínek
Fagervik, Sweden

8,175 Likes

The University of Nebraska has developed a genetically modified breed of cattle that is impervious to Tornados. As the wind speed increases, the cow's centre of gravity lowers. It eventually reaches a point that the cow cannot be lifted off the ground.

#donthaveacowman #steakyourlifeonit

Felicienne Begin
Aura, Finland

775,105 Likes

Under new EU proposals, children's "teenage" years will be altered to run from 15 to 22.

#theygrowupsofast #stupidkids

Marat Bazarov
La Pedrera, Uruguay

490,268 Likes

The humble toad is both the official animal and language of Luxembourg.

#toadsaregross #sorryIdontspeaktoad

Mario Strauss
Borgdorf-Seedorf, Germany

725,997 Likes

Seville in Spain is twinned with Bracknell Leisure Centre, Primark in Bolton and actress Miriam Margolyes.

#afineactress #thanksforthemarmalade

Eulalie Authier
Presandães, Portugal

860,892 Likes

The popular Estonian nursery rhyme "Tabanud Vanaema Kepiga" translates literally into English as "How come your Grandmother always looks at you as though she's about to murder you".

#betterthanringaringaroses
#youllmissherwhenshesgone

Mateja Marija Beke
Phoenix, United States

174,104 Likes

To protect themselves from invasion during the 2nd World War, the citizens of Poland built a wall surrounding the country, made entirely of cardboard. This was a great success until it rained.

#itsgoodbutitsnotright
#takeitonDragonsDen

Kisanet Habte
Ermesinde, Portugal

75,027 Likes

In Liechtenstein, the most common cause of death is boredom.

#nowonder #Igotboredjustspellingit

Tuva Folgerø
Reykjavík, Iceland

685,962 Likes

In 2015, Portugal held an amnesty, allowing citizens to hand in unlicensed Nerf Guns.

#youllhavesomeoneseyeout
#pray4Roraldo

Tú Hàn
Vuti, Estonia

196,326 Likes

Until 1244, radishes were worshipped as Gods in parts of Eastern Ireland.

#therealtroubles #growyourown

John Jeremiassen
Hólmavík, Iceland

345,361 Likes

The inventor of the computer keyboard was the Bulgarian Physicist, Qwerty Uiop.

#Iseewhatyoudid #Qwertytohismates

Doroteo Costa
St. Magdalen, Austria

517,297 Likes

In 1998, North Korea announced it had started developing weapons grade dominoes.

#lovedthe90s #QuiGonJinn

Brenda Pereira
Ghin Ghin, Australia

109,208 Likes

There is no word in the Albanian language for 'cat'. They simply refer to it as "that pet which is not a dog".

#servesthemright #mansworstfriend

庭碩 康
Petrolina, Brazil

489,379 Likes

Since 1985, there has been a secret operation to relocate the Falkland Islands closer to the British mainland. Buckets of soil and rocks are dug up from the south of the islands and deposited on the north shore. Over the past 32 years, they have moved 7 feet north.

#allingoodtime #Thatcherismgonemad

 Yves D'Aubigné
Schlag, Austria

974,261 Likes

To reduce the melting of the polar ice caps, massive panes of double glazing are being installed to help keep the heat out.

#letstalkmoney #windowofopportunity

 Sarah Paulsen
Kraków, Poland

74,235 Likes

In Nevada, it is illegal to put anything other than beer onto a beer mat.

#thecluesinthename
#youhavetherighttoremainsilent

 Leifur Arnarsson
Villabona, Spain

650,903 Likes

Belgians are unable to wink.

#flirtingisimpossible
#nudgenudgenothingnothing

Venera Folliero
Lappeenranta, Finland

541,816 Likes

The Turkish alphabet has only 4 letters. Variety is given to the language by simply writing the letters in different fonts.

#fontofallknowledge #cantgowrongwithCalibri

Hippolyte Glazkov
Upper Bingara, Australia

207,357 Likes

Feng Shui is Malaysian for "I don't like it there, Dear".

#canIgetsomericewiththat #blessthismess

Rashid Khadzhiyev
São Paulo, Brazil

430,884 Likes

On the Greek island of Lesbos, children are outnumbered 6 to 1 by pineapples.

#rumoursabound #amazingonpizza

Jackson Byrnes
Pofadder, South Africa

257,456 Likes

Blu-tack is classified as a Class B substance in Chad.

#verymoreish #stickthehabit

Katu Arriaga
Donkerbroek, Netherlands

127,364 Likes

The Potuskys, an extinct tribe of Eskimos, died out as they had no phrase for "Look out, here comes a polar bear".

#andyet50wordsforsnow #trysomedeicer

Victor Fredriksen
Egkomi, Cyprus

408,755 Likes

The first child in space was 9-year-old American, Tyler Woodruff. He went up in 1968 with the team from Apollo 7 and can clearly be heard in the broadcasts every 15 seconds asking, "Are we there yet?"

#hesuptherenow #kidssaythedarndestthings

子倩 鄧
Kolila, Estonia

55,855 Likes

The Moroccan city of Rabat has just elected a Pokemon Go as its new mayor.

#gottaelectthemall #IonlyknowPikachu

Joonas Salama
Lapinheira, Portugal

39,035 Likes

Prime numbers are frowned upon in Slovakia.

#notprimetime #showsomerespect

Nicola Giordano
Szczecin, Poland

391,476 Likes

The Greenwich time signal is being relocated to Paris. This means, for example, the 10 o'clock pips will be heard at 11 o'clock and people will have to adjust accordingly.

#doesnttimefly #timeforchange

Muyassar Sarraf
Björna, Sweden

135,386 Likes

The hills above the capital city of Alaska were once home to the world's largest ship building firm. Hence the city's name, Anchor-Ridge.

#fakedAlaska
#thishopeisananchorformysoul

Umut Beijk
Patreksfjörður, Iceland

382,854 Likes

All Mexicans are born left-handed.

#leftbehind #Illberightback

Da-Xia Yang
Cervera del Maestre, Spain

900,469 Likes

Eskimos have 50 different words for Dermot O'Leary. None of them affectionate.

#seemsabitexcessive #hedoeshisbest

Edvina Draginc
Klein-Jetzelsdorf, Austria

614,945 Likes

In Arkansas, it is still legal to marry a pig, provided that pig is a confirmed virgin.

#pulledpork #prettyinpink

Марта Александрова
Sandgerði, Iceland

47,213 Likes

The 'get out of jail free' card from Monopoly is transferable to all real-life jails in El Salvador.

#playtowin #prisonrules

Oscar Landrø
Pori, Finland

576,827 Likes

In Lithuania, the word 'Goodbye' got overused and wore out in the late 1960's. Since then, at the end of conversations locals have just shrugged and sloped off.

#smellyoulater #OKbyethen

Marine Mota
Wrocław, Poland

936,741 Likes

The Sicilian mafia started as a Neighbourhood Watch, but quickly got out of hand.

#funnyhow #Imgonnamakehimalemonsponge hecantrefuse

匠 末本
West Bundaleer, Australia

338,368 Likes

The Battle of Waterloo was named after the famous ABBA song, which the Duke of Wellington was listening to continuously on his I-pod during the conflict.

#thewinnertakesitall #tuuuuuuuunnnnnnne

 Vinícius Cardoso
Mesogi, Cyprus

203,243 Likes

The city of Jerusalem was originally named Kevin, after the actor Kevin Costner.

#cityofdreams #ifyoubuildit

 Božena Šichová
Teuva, Finland

141,223 Likes

French novelist Voltaire made a fortune on the side by harvesting calf livers. His finest work, Candide, was originally entitled 'How I made a fortune harvesting and selling calf livers.'

#donthaveacowman #anovelidea

 Egberto Esquibel
Washington, United States

721,655 Likes

The Tet Offensive during the Vietnam War was due to be called "Happy Funtime Good", but this was deemed inappropriate.

#backtothedrawingboard
#nowthatsoffensive

Lok Liu
Mühlhausen, Germany

396,993 Likes

All London black cabs are grade 2 listed.

#historicLondon #savedforthenation

Eve Flakelar
Αραδιππου, Cyprus

758,800 Likes

The Docklands Light Railway was built by Hornby, as a full-size development of the r Scalextric range.

#boystoys #weallpretendtodrive

実 園山
Kallavere, Estonia

143,267 Likes

The Woolwich Ferry once spent 4 weeks in the Betty Ford clinic to overcome an antifreeze addiction.

#dryingout #seekhelp

สุไพรระหง สุวรรณสะอาด
Kostelec nad Cernými Lesy, Czech Republic

694,581 Likes

Euro Tunnel has two main running tunnels. The one for trains to France is measured in kilometres. The one coming to England is measured in miles.

#twosystems #checkyourtapemeasure

Heike Eichelberger
Meadow Lake, Canada

770,336 Likes

If you placed every branch of Subway in London next to each other, they would be exactly the same length as the Bakerloo line.

#neverknewthat #changehereforlunch

宛妤 程
Roure, Italy

177,123 Likes

The original railway station at Redhill in Surrey, was built using just bamboo.

#pandafriendly #cheapestoption

Bucca Bunce
Arnhem, Netherlands

397,179 Likes

The Dockland Light Railway gets its name from the original plan, where the trains were to run using Solar Power.

#sunny #blameMichaelFish

家茜 彭
Walliswil bei Niederbipp, Switzerland

527,261 Likes

A Sat-Nav coding error has been discovered in the latest devices. If people are travelling along the A3 and actually wanted to go along the A4, they are simply advised to fold the road in half.

#makessense #teardownthedottedline

Else Kleist
Gerard, Australia

182,490 Likes

To ease parking congestion in London, drivers will be able to park their cars on Underground station platforms outside of peak hours.

#mindthegap #didunothat

 Iselin Markussen
Nîmes, France

767,225 Likes

The Doppler Effect, where noise frequency drops as a vehicle passes you, has been proven to be a myth. Vehicles with sirens simply have buttons on the dashboard that allow the driver to reduce the pitch as he passes you.

#madeup #pushthebutton

 Mek Hurgoh
Pretoria, South Africa

753,244 Likes

The widening of a 5 mile stretch of the M23 has been awarded to the 3rd Crawley Brownie pack.

#dibdibdig #givethemabadge

 Joachim Møller
Cite El Intilaka, Tunisia

138,390 Likes

The M3 in Hampshire is to lose its Smart Motorway status after failing the 11-plus.

#thicko #extralessons

Shakirah Almasi
Assendelft, Netherlands

99,044 Likes

In 2022, the Dockland Light Railway will be extended to reach fictional destinations, such as Albert Square, Narnia and Brigadoon.

#servingeveryone #getouttamypub

 نیوشا مدرس
Τρεμιθουσα, Cyprus

448,796 Likes

To cover for vital upgrade works at the National Railway Museum in York, a temporary National Bus Replacement Museum will be set up in the car park.

#refurbishment #waitforages

 Larissa Souza
Drebkau, Germany

159,746 Likes

To increase capacity on the London Underground, new lines are to be placed in disused sewage pipes. Passengers will need to lie down in order to fit.

#keepLondoninmotion #urinetrouble

 Anna Mikkelsen
Loutra Tis Afroditis, Cyprus

651,009 Likes

Former Top Gear presenter Richard Hammond has a phobia about the Bakerloo line and must be tranquillized before going on it.

#sleepyhamster #dontlethimdrive

# Heiðbjört Harðardóttir
Valencia, Spain

890,552 Likes

If you travel clockwise on the Circle line, starting from Aldgate. all the stations are in alphabetical order.

#ocd #gottohaveasystem

Lukasz McKay
Carlos Reyles, Uruguay

430,115 Likes

To stop people running when the food is available, all self-service wedding buffets now come fitted with speed bumps.

#slowdownNigel #foodcalmingmeasures

Prima Fairbairn
Abersky, United Kingdom

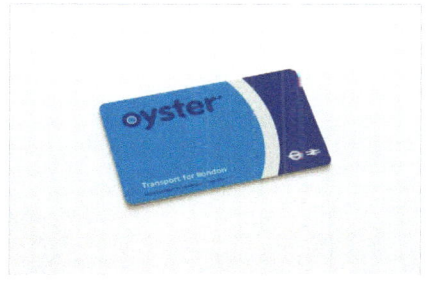

56,951 Likes

New pedestrian only lanes are to be introduced in London's Oxford street to allow people to get through crowds of shoppers. Walkers will have to tap in and out using their oyster cards.

#beatthesystem #keepmoving

良子 榊田
Vattholma, Sweden

940,252 Likes

The original plan for the M25 was for it to have no off-ramps. This was to reduce congestion in the rest of London by trapping cars round the outside.

#gotcha #roundandround

Heike Zimmerman
Romanens, Switzerland

305,351 Likes

At Tottenham Court Road underground station, to avoid queues, customers will be given the chance to slide down the section between the escalators on a doormat.

#wheeee #standontherightplease

Bilqiz Barsukov
Γεραvι, Cyprus

400,203 Likes

Chalfont & Latimer Underground Station has been announced as one of the contestants on this year's "I'm A Celebrity Get Me Out of Here".

#opentoall #Ant&Dec

苡含 黃
Skamby, Denmark

815,085 Likes

All cars can transform into fighting robots. Most of them are just lazy.

#whatsthisbuttondo #cantbebothered

 **Arkhip Matveyev**
Hallormsstaður, Iceland

710,280 Likes

From next May, as well as sign language and subtitles, the BBC will be translating the news into interpretive dance.

#strictlyconfidential #BritishBreakdancingCorporation

 Théophile Proulx
Palma Campania, Italy

329,846 Likes

All sports shown by Sky Sports actually take place on the Isle of Skye.

#seemslegit #blueSkyethinking

 Shadin Mifsud
Te Atatu South, New Zealand

40,426 Likes

When played backwards, the 2012 Christmas episode of TV show Miranda contains a hidden message in Urdu.

#yuleloveit #stilleasiertocomprehendthanMrsBrownsBoys

 Darko Marinović
Germiston, South Africa

522,273 Likes

The TV series Blackadder Goes Forth has never been translated for overseas listeners. It was recorded using an audio system which means viewers automatically hear it in their own language.

#whatacunningplan #maybewarisntallbad

大輝 舟川
Kouvola, Finland

261,945 Likes

Actress June Whitfield put her longevity down to being powered by 12 triple-A batteries.

#ageshallnotwearyher #Iflippinglovescience

 Nicolas Cardoso
Dravograd, Slovenia

813,053 Likes

90's pop group "The Farm" funded their single "All Together Now" via an EU subsidy.

#arable #fallowseasonsince1994

 Senapus Berger
Leiden, Netherlands

718,835 Likes

The film Watership Down was written as a comedy by an author who just didn't like rabbits.

#andwhocanblamehim #getastewgoing

 Izaak Szczepański
Pregartsdorf, Austria

33,149 Likes

Former weatherman Ian McCaskill played the role of 3rd racist from the left in the 1994 film, "The Shawshank Redemption."

#checksIMDB #nomakeuprequired

Leonor Fernandes
Molare, Italy

768,933 Likes

Kebab shops were introduced into the UK in 1976, as part of Turkish reparations for the UK winning the Eurovision Song Contest that year.

#organdoner #youcanhavethembacknow

Kheldas Nivalli
Vilar do Pinheiro, Portugal

917,503 Likes

The BBC has admitted that old tapes of "Keeping Up Appearances" have started breeding whilst unattended. 98 new episodes will reach full maturity by next Easter.

#thelacyofthehousespeaking #sexy

Ludvig Lundblad
Pietersburg, South Africa

584,712 Likes

The BBC has announced that, for the next series of Strictly Come Dancing, twerking will be added to the list of dances.

#Brunosidea #keepmodernising

Owen King
Λευκωσια, Cyprus

165,016 Likes

ITV has announced a new Saturday night TV series. Members of the public will compete for a chance to join the Football Pools Panel.

#hostedbyPaddyMcGuinnessprobs #bringbackGladiators

Kalitta Jarov
Qaanaaq, Greenland

793,421 Likes

For 3 series, no one noticed that the Blue Peter tortoise was actually a novelty shaped doorstop.

#aboutasinteresting
#theprayerthatJesustortoise

 Helen Yonatan
Ladysmith, South Africa

778,439 Likes

The TV show Rentaghost is still the most popular programme in the Dominican Republic.

#spookyfact #Ilovethe80s

 Jayne Blankenstijn
Kraków, Poland

582,541 Likes

The lyrics to Bohemian Rhapsody were created by using the game Boggle to come up with each word, one at a time.

#tryPictionarynexttime
#cantdotheFandango

 ดาริกา บุญฐานะ
Κανλι, Cyprus

200,363 Likes

Musical one hit wonders Babylon Zoo have revealed that the band was forced to split up after failing animal welfare tests.

#dontfeedthem #therewerenosurvivors

拓海 矢次
Obergegend, Austria

341,975 Likes

S Club 7 are the UK most successful pop act named after a chocolate biscuit.

#theSstandsforslippery #Paulatethelot

 Ринат Волошин
Charneca de Caparica, Portugal

889,782 Likes

After his death, 80's puppet Spit the Dog was recycled into a novelty doorstop.

#deathisstillamystery
#mayGodhavemercyonhissoul

 Luisana Enriquez
Redwoodtown, New Zealand

668,734 Likes

To highlight how poor some British Radio had become, a station was set up last year that transmitted nothing but silence, 24 hours a day. After 3 months, it had twice as many listeners as Matt Richardson on Virgin Drivetime.

#seriousjoking #whatisthisthe1800s

 Guaraci Suárez
Eckernförde, Germany

716,435 Likes

Timmy Mallett is the first Children's TV Presenter to be given Grade 1 listed status.

#NationalTrust #saveourMallett

Lupčo Kurunič
Gittisham, United Kingdom

746,872 Likes

Charles Darwin invented Stickle Bricks.

#survivalofthesticklest #evolutionnotrevolution

 Ante Herceg
Vitória, Brazil

180,551 Likes

Sir James Dyson has invented the Ambidextrous Clock, which can show the hours or minutes with either hand.

#timeonhishands #abitclocky

 Alberta Padovesi
St Louisville, United States

641,195 Likes

Former Chancellor George Osbourne used to be a personal bodyguard for the Why Don't You presenters.

#amanofmanytalents #politicsnotoneofthem

 Эрика Блинова
Risabus, United Kingdom

69,814 Likes

In the upcoming stage adaptation of "GMTV – The Musical", the part of Piers Morgan is to be played by Wee Jimmy Krankie.

#perfectcasting #endofthePiers

Flora Zubareva
Drávaszentes, Hungary

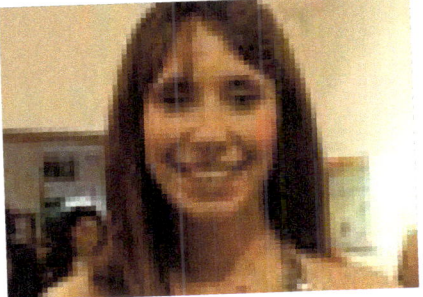

706,293 Likes

"One Show" presenter Alex Jones was the 2009 Welsh parkour champion.

#nicelittlerunaround
#CharlotteChurchgotbronze

Esa-Pekka Hietamäki
Oum Jenna, Tunisia

22,335 Likes

MC Hammer's full name is Mitchell Clarence Hammerenstein.

#cantspellthis #nailedit

Denis Danielsson
Siglufjörður, Iceland

699,209 Likes

Another big budget Hollywood remake will hit our screens next year. The live action version of Captain Scarlet will star Mel Gibson in the title role, with British comedian Joe Pasquale providing the voice of the Mysterons.

#PasqualeoftheChrist
#highpitchediswellpitched

Галина Коровина
Station Nord, Greenland

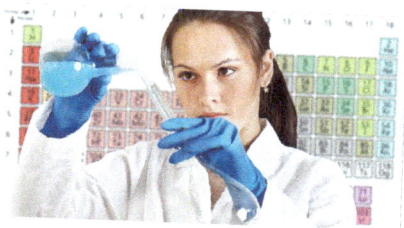

125,063 Likes

A new reality TV program will aim to simplify the Periodic Table. The show, "I'm A Low Conductive Metalloid, Get Me Out Of Here", will give qualified chemists the chance to vote off their least favoured elements.

#boxsetbinge #carbonneutral

Артур Булгаков
Rahinge, Estonia

10,046 Likes

The thirteenth series of the X-Factor finished in a tie. The winner was decided by a game of "British Bulldog".

#itsnotstillonisit #Xcellentplaygroundgame

Eliza Ponebšek
Ostrava 28, Czech Republic

820,270 Likes

When it says at the end of the credits 'no animals were harmed in the making of this', that is always a joke.

#comedygold #slaughteredformeat

Abbie Burke
Scafati, Italy

970,503 Likes

Megatron was the name they chose for the leader of the Decepticons when the original name, Ian, was ruled out.

#notafanofchange #allhailian

Borna Razpotnik
Καλο Χωριο Λαρνακας, Cyprus

831,403 Likes

More actors have been in Casualty than have been in actual casualty.

#castofmillions #saveourNHS

 **Labid Gaber**
Amargeti, Cyprus

635,331 Likes

Goodfellas starring Ray Liotta is actually the prequel to the Disney Pixar smash, UP.

#difficultsecondalbum #funnyhow

 Matilda Hindmarsh
Cerro Chato, Uruguay

374,537 Likes

For the film Inception, Christopher Nolan approached 90's band D:ream about providing the score. He felt that would be appropriate.

#nailedit #thingsdidntgetbetter

 Ari-Pekka Mäkelä
La Palma del Condado, Spain

472,895 Likes

There was a 2-week gap during the writing of Macbeth, after Shakespeare's computer crashed.

#thecurseoftheScottishplay
#writeonMacduff

 Romolo Angelo
Perlesreut, Germany

495,953 Likes

The filming of Disney's The Jungle Book was held up when a family of tourists inadvertently walked onto set and were subsequently mauled to death by Baloo.

#bearwithus #maybeDisneyisntallgoodthen

Awwab Shammas
Sulz, Austria

879,340 Likes

One famous scene from Lord of The Rings was filmed in Matalan's Hartlepool branch. If you look carefully over Gimli's shoulder, you can see a slightly confused member of staff called Dean, radioing for security.

#youshallnotpasstheunderwearsection #mypreciousdiscountstore

 Charlotte Karlsen
Kristiansand S, Norway

493,027 Likes

The Swiss government sent a letter to the makers of "24", bemoaning the fact that they weren't considered evil enough to be considered villains. 'We're sick of being the neutrals. Why should the Koreans get all the fun? We hate America, it's just that nobody ever listens to us.'

#cheeseandclocks #stuckinneutral

 Tore Andersson
Nodebais, Belgium

125,025 Likes

Wall.E. was first choice to play Batman, but Christian Bale locked him in a shed on the morning of the auditions.

#whysoserious #notactuallybornagain

 Andwise Grubb
Pinehill, New Zealand

640,277 Likes

There was a 5th Beatle, Colin, who lived in Ringo's bass drum and played the Marimba on 'Til there was you'.

#historywrittenbythewinners #weloveyouColin

Vignette Guay
Cergy, France

13,188 Likes

The boyband 5ive broke up when Ab's plans to open a cheese hamlet were scuppered by J.

#slamdunkdastilton #everyBcursingetup

 Chiemezie Chukwufumnanya
Profitis Ilias, Cyprus

762,103 Likes

In the original stage performance of the Lion King, a real Lion was used to portray "Scar". Tragically, during "Hakuna Matata", the Lion leapt into the orchestra pit, killing both oboe players and a saxophonist.

#junglemusic #classicDisney

 Simone Schröder
Stavanger, Norway

975,042 Likes

After the success of Y.M.C.A., the Village People tried a similar ploy with a song entitled B+M Bargains. It was a commercial failure.

#aheadoftheirtime
#myfavouritewasthecowboy

 Idzi Woźniak
Torphichen, United Kingdom

542,526 Likes

If you listen to any Katy Perry song backwards, you can clearly hear the words 'Your life is worthless'.

#yourenotafirework #IpreferPerryMason

Home & Garden

Branka Kuprešak
Rümlingen, Switzerland

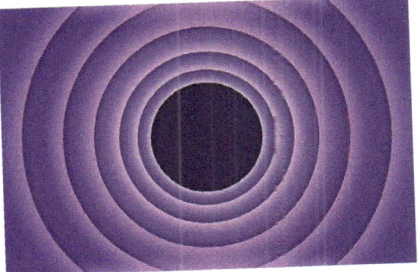

♥ 💬

648,144 Likes

All DIY shops put mauve paint in a separate aisle. This dates back to when it started.

#wevealwaysdoneitlikethat #marooned

Imogen Forster
Velika Nedelja, Slovenia

♥ 💬

76,258 Likes

From next year, Waitrose will allow customers to download smoked salmon directly to their fridges.

#thatshandyTarquin #poshgrub

Юлия Егорова
Matosinhos, Portugal

 💬

962,142 Likes

If you pretend to eat a jalapeno pepper, you start to sweat behind your ears.

#allinthemind #haveyougotatissue

Sai Uchiyama
Tiszarád, Hungary

♥ 💬

571,219 Likes

It is predicted that, with the advent of smart chip technology, wheelie bins will become self-aware by the year 2050.

#Skynetrecycling #rubbishAlexa

 **Tibor Fehér**
Gif-Sur-Yvette, France

617,670 Likes

Potato croquettes are simply obese chips.

#fattyfood #OMGbmi

 Shahrazad Daher
Strovolos, Cyprus

344,995 Likes

Corned Beef is now classified as a class B substance. You can receive up to 3 months in prison for possession.

#wannabuyasandwich #raidthebutchers

 Rafaela Cavalcanti
Schneeberg, Germany

781,970 Likes

The Buddhist custom of leaving a meringue in your coal scuttle dates back to 1724.

#lostinthemistsoftime #itsatradition

 Tamara Kuncz
Utrecht, Netherlands

580,110 Likes

Chicken and Mushroom Pot Noodle has been reclassified as a Class A substance.

#justaddwater #nottobesniffedat

政國 史
Canelón Grande Represa, Uruguay

818,498 Likes

Do you know where the term jacket potato comes from? Irish farmers used to save the skins from their potatoes and sewed them together to make rudimentary clothing. This process is still in use today making clothes for George at Asda.

#losthistory #organicclothing

Livia Fernandes
Sandefjord, Norway

720,151 Likes

Drystone walls are like normal stone walls, just completely teetotal.

#teetotal #designatedboundarymarker

Blanco Whitfoot
Kunda, Estonia

754,942 Likes

From 2019, a pack of playing cards will expand to 65 with the addition of a new suit, Granite.

#makepokerharder #trickytodealwith

Milislava Bravič
Åsensbruk, Sweden

589,053 Likes

A new range of upper case Alphabetti Spaghetti is being produced for short sighted people.

#squintypasta #needabiggertin

L'Tava Qarmduct
Dol pri Hrastniku, Slovenia

998,662 Likes

Garden sheds were saved from extinction by cross breeding dog kennels with garages.

#conservation #dilutethegenepool

 Guillermina Gaytan
Λευκωσια, Cyprus

170,741 Likes

The bendy straw was invented in 1968 by M People lead singer, Heather Small.

#neverknewthat #sucker

 Tapa Kadyrov
Nancy, France

350,548 Likes

Trade Union law dictates that a person cannot be a shop steward unless they live in a flat over a shop.

#makessensenow #everybodyout

 Michelle Pfeiffer
Betheln, Germany

719,470 Likes

On average, it takes 4 months to housetrain a wild flower.

#breakthemin #domesticatedflora

Tekashishikutata
Ranui Heights, New Zealand

944,096 Likes

From next year, Alphabetti Spaghetti will be available to buy in a range of different fonts.

#expandtherange #yummyWingdings

Rong Kung
Bernburg, Germany

539,922 Likes

Cavity wall insulation is made from recycled beer mats.

#reuse #dontspillmyinsulation

Lubanah Naifeh
Toronto, Canada

693,403 Likes

The welcome mat was invented by former boxer Prince Naseem Hamed.

#bighit #wipeyourfeet

Cang Cao
Dole, France

877,841 Likes

Trilby hats were originally feral. However, they died out in the wild in 1955, leaving only the domesticated variety we know today.

#endangeredheadwear #naturalworld

Murron Cunningham
Appleton, United States

400,222 Likes

On a standard computer keyboard, there is a thin gap between the F4 & F5 buttons. This is because the original layout developer of a keyboard, wanted somewhere to rest his Pepperami.

#snacks #itsabitofananimal

Henrik Filemonsen
Rask Mølle, Denmark

583,387 Likes

The pencil sharpener was invented in 1885 by Genesis keyboard player, Tony Banks.

#sideline #gettothepoint

مهناز خاتمی
Reykjavík, Iceland

40,689 Likes

The Bic Biro was introduced to the UK in 1907 from Egypt. The subsequent population explosion has forced the native crayon to the edge of extinction.

#cullthepens #didntseethatcoming

Max Uhr
Kirchlindach, Switzerland

549,264 Likes

When people who are hosting dinner parties say they've prepared nibbles and canapes what they really mean is 'I couldn't be arsed to do a pizza'.

#lazy #twoforTuesday

Louie Fraser
Dordrecht, Netherlands

513,640 Likes

Using words like nibbles and canapes instantly makes you middle class. Also 'proper coffee'.

#wellspoken #niceneighbourhood

Hannah Lauritsen
Miami, United States

315,987 Likes

Tents are, by their very nature, nervous structures.

#worried #tellmeaboutyourmother

Yasuka Nakashima
Alluitsup Paa, Greenland

377,141 Likes

The man who invented the mug did so shortly after trying to use his hands to cup boiling hot tea.

#ouch #holdthisforme

بزرگمهر شاهدباز
Ypäjä, Finland

268,144 Likes

PG Tips do actually hand out handy hints inside their products and led one man from Scarborough to set up his own gritting business.

#teasolveseverything #ontheroadtoajob

Yu Jie Feng
El Achach, Tunisia

723,309 Likes

Mattel, the makers of Scrabble, are allowing players the chance to neaten up the game board, by launching their own range of scrabble tile grout.

#DIYgames #stillnonamesthough

Nico Dahl
Uddebo, Sweden

77,474 Likes

People whose name begins with the letter S are 3 times more likely to be imprisoned for forgery than any other letter.

#wasthatyouSteve #goingdown

Jakov Horvat
Berlicum, Netherlands

117,330 Likes

From next year, the alphabet will be reduced to 25 letters when the letter Q is abolished.

#simplification #beattheq

Đinh Hà
Canelas, Portugal

513,975 Likes

Darkness travels at the speed of light, only in the opposite direction.

#makessense #equalandoppositereaction

 **Rion Inaba**
Μαμωνια, Cyprus

441,226 Likes

When heated to exactly 73 degrees Celsius, Coconuts become invisible to the naked eye.

#scienceisamazing #cantseeitworking

 Ryan Costa
Bentley, United Kingdom

305,427 Likes

The Custard Crème has retained its title as the world's most aerodynamic biscuit for a record 12th straight year.

#championsnack #flieswell

 Cailey Roks
Kralovice, Czech Republic

669,217 Likes

The Rubik's Cube has been proven to lower cholesterol in the over 60's.

#healthygame #keepfit

 Togo Twofoot
Wancennes, Belgium

915,377 Likes

Neon is the first element of the periodic table to have dual British and Irish citizenship.

#international #sheddinglightonit

Kagran Kotzher
Corcelles-près-Payerne, Switzerland

709,032 Likes

If you take half an avocado and plunge into a bowl of tepid water, it will get wet.

#butofcourse #whatdidyouexpect

 Valerie Fedorov
Rümikon Switzerland

504,460 Likes

High fibre broadband counts as one of your 5 a day.

#quicktips #onlinediets

 Makar Butusov
Uljaste, Estonia

539,529 Likes

Due to a typing error, the latest WWF list of endangered species now includes Rhubarb Crumble.

#endangeredpuddings #oops

 國安 何
Station Nord, Greenland

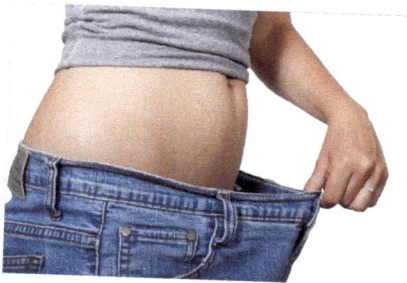

285,613 Likes

Weight Watchers have proposed that people are so used to diets failing; they should not be called diets anymore. Now, they are suggesting calling them Obesity Erosion Schemes

#politicallycorrect #dontgetoffended

Iole Mancini
Harrau, Austria

523,484 Likes

In order to arrest overweight people, the Police are trialling a new range of stingers that are covered with fun sized chocolate bars, rather than spikes.

#beatthemattheirowngame #tempting

Mikael Davidsen
Šoštanj, Slovenia

342,844 Likes

Possession of a packet of Space Raiders crisps can still be punished with a 7-day jail sentence.

#keepthestreetssafe
#noonelikesthemanyway

Ulrich Wannemaker
Campinas, Brazil

487,442 Likes

Professional hermit Arthur Boswell has lived in an en-suite bathroom at 11 Downing Street for the last 28 years.

#longtermresident #partofthefurniture

Will Proudfoot
Kansas City, United States

889,283 Likes

In pre-decimal bibles, there are 360 psalms.

#oldentimes #praiseHimonthefractions

Adelgrim Chubb-Baggins
Canworthy Water, United Kingdom

842,828 Likes

The price of a second class post-it note has risen to 38p.

#howmuch #stickyproblem

Taziana Bianchi
Bergen, Norway

81,280 Likes

Prior to 1923, a pack of playing cards contained 56 cards, not 52. Each suit had the numbers 2 to 10, plus the Ace, King, Queen, Jack and Mr Bun the Baker.

#ishehighorlow #facedoutofuse

Tesmi Futsum
Klobuky v Cechách, Czech Republic

695,509 Likes

The trumpet is the only musical instrument in the world that can play the note of H. To make the note, you hold down all three keys and suck in violently.

#musicalknowledge #andbreathe

สุนทีทิพย์ สัธนะกุล
Tulešice, Czech Republic

989,364 Likes

Although it appears to be an incomplete 4 story building, the headquarters of the creators of Tetris should be the tallest building in the world at over 347 stories. It was just that, whenever the builders completed an entire floor, it disappeared.

#haventyoufinishedyet #wherediditgo

Laura Ryan
Sabiote, Spain

916,258 Likes

There has been an 89% increase in the sale of the "Trom". This is perfect for people who love brass instruments but prefer them filleted in the shop to remove the bone.

#popularmusic #savesmethebother

Melampus Zaragamba
Rillieux-La-Pape, France

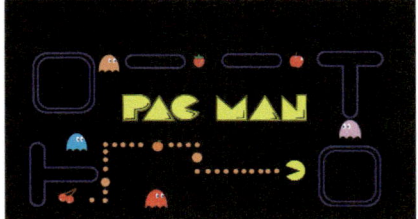

745,589 Likes

In 1988, a petition to ban the practice of hunting Pac-Man gained over 96,000 signatures.

#cruelty #voiceofthepeople

Archibald Douglas
Hillegom, Netherlands

581,414 Likes

A ruling by the Supreme Court, now allows pecks of pickled peppers to be picked by persons of any name, not just those called Peter Piper.

#opentoall #whatsapeckanyway

Barry Rochon
Westerland, Netherlands

84,999 Likes

To reduce costs, the year 2022 will only be 358 days long. This will be achieved by the abolition of 14 consecutive Tuesday afternoons.

#timespassingquickly #losttrackoftime

Liva Hansen
Castel San Pietro Romano, Italy

118,726 Likes

From next June, the Times Crossword will become 3-dimensional. Clues will be categorised as Across, Down and Away.

#needabiggerpaper #headscratcher

Hildifons Maggot
Bello Horizonte, Uruguay

137,199 Likes

The term "Blue Sky Thinking" has been labelled as offensive, by the British Colour Blindness Association.

#dontupsetthem #wordshavepower

郁婷 曹
Warren, United States

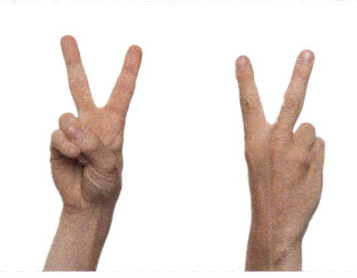

956,588 Likes

The British Medical Association has claimed that people who give rude hand gestures are actually suffering from a form of non-verbal Tourette's.

#canthelpthemselves #howmanyfingers

Xuyến Lưu
Maribor, Slovenia

884,480 Likes

Since 1974, the use of meaningless percentages has gone up by over 263%.

#importantstats #knewi-

 **Chang Yeh**
Húsavík, Iceland

267,636 Likes

From the start of next year, Capital letters are to be replaced by Emoji's.

#modernways #languagemoveson

 Luana Ferreira
Stalham, United Kingdom

51,289 Likes

Scientists are warning about the danger of reflected daylight at night-time and are advising anyone out after dark to wear Moon Cream.

#safetyfirst #dontburninbed

 Alejandrina Noriega
Vollen, Norway

913,959 Likes

Fast food chain Greggs is working on the first virtual reality steak bake. Customers will be able to eat them in any wi-fi enabled shop.

#downloadable #techyfood

 Chí Trịnh
Green Range, Australia

254,976 Likes

The Kama Sutra is more relaxed than its twin publication, the Intense Sutra.

#chillout #interestingpositions

Csombor Sultés
Rotokauri, New Zealand

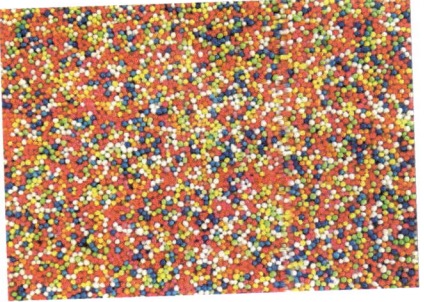

205,248 Likes

Because of rampant inflation, the ice cream topping "hundreds and thousands" is to be renamed "millions and billions".

#costsmore #wantaflakewiththat

和也 秋友
Lyon, France

91,947 Likes

Following a crash in the share price, a 99 Ice Cream will now be known as a 68.

#notworthitanymore #Illhavealolly

Ali Petrie
Bälinge, Sweden

320,574 Likes

Following a court case around discrimination, Little Chef is to be rebranded as Vertically Challenged Cookery Operative.

#dontupsetthem #shortfuse

Jeppe Clausen
Cachovice u Mladé Boleslave, Czech Republic

452,668 Likes

Of all the elements in the periodic table, Calcium is the only one that is left-handed.

#talented #uniqueproperties

Chiemezie Eluemuno
Morden, Canada

528,573 Likes

As part of new inclusivity laws, street Mime Artists now must come with subtitles.

#whatdidhejustsay #braillenext

آزاده مرادی
Utö, Sweden

157,343 Likes

The 5-2 diet was so named, as people could only eat food 5 minutes prior to the end of each hour.

#watchtheclock #cramitinquick

Pavel Svoboda
Askim, Norway

721,049 Likes

After 2026, all French Fries will be deported.

#sendemhome #takingbackcontrol

Božidar Stanković
Villamena, Spain

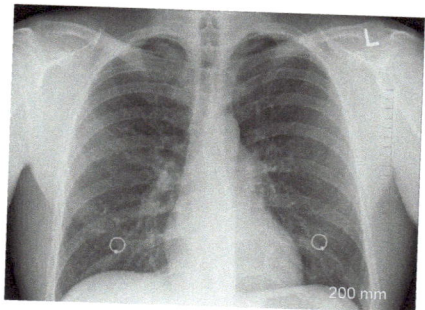

11,687 Likes

Pneumonia was invented in 1944 after humans became immune to the original "monia", or "Oldmonia" as it is now called.

#updatingillness #medicinemoveson

優太 江坂
Edgeware, New Zealand

720,715 Likes

Do you know why humans have evolved without the ability to lick their own elbows? The sweat from the human elbow is poisonous.

#natureprotectsus #couldkillyou

 Milena Málková
Nové Mesto nad Metují 1, Czech Republic

542,235 Likes

The Kinder Surprise was named after its inventor, Marcus Surprise.

#makessense #genius

 Mitsuaki Haraguchi
Vihti, Finland

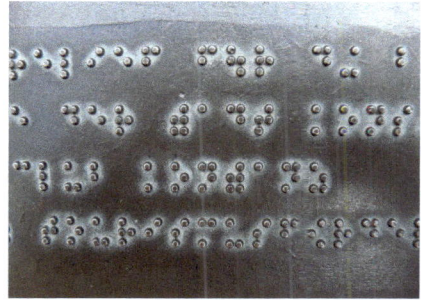

205,223 Likes

To help visually impaired people, all silent letters, such as the "P" in Psalm or the "H" in Ghost will now have to pronounced in braille.

#shush #speakingtheirlanguage

 Demetria Genovesi
Nossebro, Sweden

213,664 Likes

Did you know that the process for skimming stones across a lake is the same one used for skimming milk? The succession of bounces on the water surface causes all the fat to rise to the top and it is then scraped off.

#healthywater #naturalprocess

Rong Ch'in
Northcross, New Zealand

135,740 Likes

Under new sarcasm laws, police can give on the spot fines to anyone they think is "being a bit lippy".

#keepyourgobshut #saynothing

 Satoe Jouon
St Cyrille De Wendover, Canada

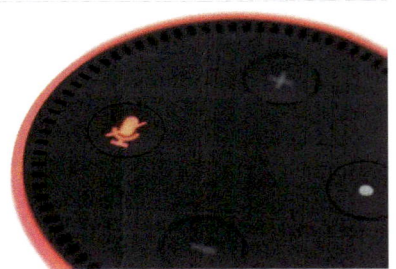

623,072 Likes

From 2024, all echos will be bi-lingual.

#inclusive #comingoverhertakingourechos

 Larissa Rodrigues
Benaocaz, Spain

969,696 Likes

From next year, people who daydream are to be fitted with answering machines.

#leaveamessage #nooneshome

 Rule Primeau
Myalla, Australia

77,657 Likes

A recent survey has shown that 143% of people think survey results are made up.

#dontbelieveyou
#proveanythingwithnumbers

Irenka Dudek
Izel, Belgium

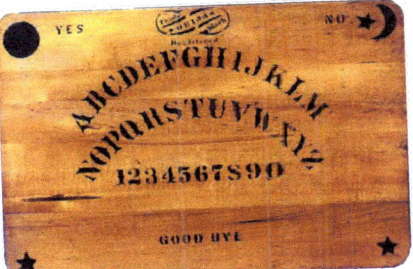

361,213 Likes

If a Ouija Board is not available, it is possible to contact the spirits on the deceased using a 1995 Argos Catalogue.

#isthatyouuncleDave #dontnickthepens

Bulat Bazhenov
Loutros, Cyprus

164,923 Likes

Lined paper is just plain paper with wrinkles.

#oldage #sameontheinside

Julian Souza
Tábor 2, Czech Republic

167,629 Likes

The Fahrenheit scale was named after its creator, Dr Nicholas Scale.

#hottopic #thanksNicky

Pavel Farský
Greenhithe, New Zealand

389,781 Likes

Green highlighter pens only work when you move them from left to right. If you go the opposite direction, nothing will come out.

#nonoeknowswhy #usefultips

海斗 沢原
Kangaatsiaq, Greenland

308,389 Likes

People who step onto an escalator with their right foot first, are 4 times more likely to win the National Lottery jackpot than those who lead with their left.

#itcouldbeyou #superstitious

Mason Icely
Saletto, Italy

473,108 Likes

As part of the drive to a paperless society, the game "Rock, Paper, Scissors" will be re-branded as "User, excel spreadsheet, helpful paper clip". User opens excel, excel wakes up paper clip, paper clip irritates user.

#cliproundtheear #updatedgames

Sophie Sharp
Paarl, South Africa

810,359 Likes

The website Trip Advisor originally gave advice on how to make it look like you hadn't tripped at all, like turning it into a little jog.

#careful #meanttodothat

Harald Kušek
Anaheim, United States

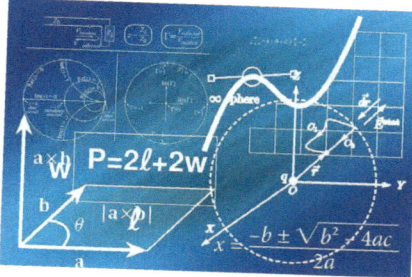

353,958 Likes

Science died for your sins.

#praiseHimonthebunsenburner #grateful

Pipaluk Lennert
Frederiksberg C, Denmark

308,254 Likes

Revenge is sweet and best served cold. Revenge is therefore ice-cream.

#logical #wantaflakewiththat

Vujo Perać
Mammendorf, Germany

331,360 Likes

Screaming "have sex with me or I'm leaving you" is the best-known aphrodisiac in the world.

#gaggingforit #helloladies

Leonardo Husikć
Kamna Gorica, Slovenia

184,248 Likes

The number 8 is openly homosexual.

#beingreal #alwayswondered

Sanna-Leen Haataja
Toronto, Canada

781,702 Likes

The letters 'u' and 'w' don't get on. Hence why the letter 'v' is there to hold them eternally apart.

#fightfightfight #gotoyourrooms

Leonardo Araujo
Augsburg, Germany

956,480 Likes

The word smelly is itself smelly, to the point that other words avoid it at social functions.

#haveashower #lifeimitatesarts

Rosalía Soto
Cite De La Poste, Tunisia

641,129 Likes

11 is bi curious.

#justwondering #whathappensif

Yolanda Clayhanger
Alphen aan den Rijn, Netherlands

24,407 Likes

If you look up the word dictionary in the dictionary, the ghost of Dr Johnson appears and cuts off your head.

#dontdoit #whoyougonnacall

Amos van Weerden
Lopera, Spain

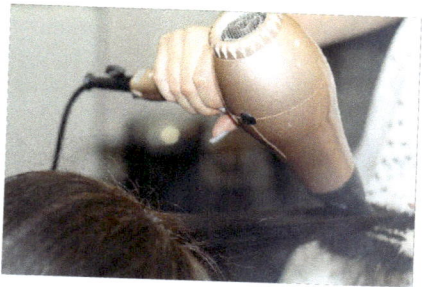

207,190 Likes

Toni and Guy, the hairdressers are also small-time mobsters and will regularly ram-raid other hairdressers in a galvanised Ford Focus.

#turfwars #cutthemdowntosize

Kyong Shipe
Aglantzia, Cyprus

147,458 Likes

The year 1756 didn't happen. It just couldn't be arsed, and so the calendar goes from 55 to 57.

#neveramounttoanything #forgetitexisted

Erotic Parsnip (p10) by daveyjane on Flickr
Used under Creative Commons License CC-BY-2.0

Lemmings (p10) by Sascha Kohlmann on Flickr
Used under Creative Commons License CC-BY-SA-2.0

Madonna (p13) by chrisweger on Flickr
Used under Creative Commons License CC-BY-SA-2.0

Wildebeest (p14) by Derek Keats on Flickr
Used under Creative Commons License CC-BY-2.0

Swindon Sign (p15) by N Chadwick on Geograph
Used under Creative Commons License CC-BY-SA-2.0

Dutch Elm Tree (p18) by Ahodges7 on Wikimedia
Used under Creative Commons License CC-BY-SA-3.0

FA Cup Trophy (p23) by Carlos yo on Wikimedia
Used under Creative Commons License CC-BY-SA-4.0

Swingball (p24) by Akuppa John Wigham on Flickr
Used under Creative Commons License CC-BY-2.0

Jon McCririck (p24) by Will Palmer on Flickr
Used under Creative Commons License CC-BY-2.0

the Dalai Lama (p24) by Luca Galuzzi on Wikimedia
Used under Creative Commons License CC-BY-SA-2.5

Wales Map (p2) by NordNordWest on Wikimedia
Used under Creative Commons License CC-BY-SA-3.0

Salt & Vinegar Crisps (p26) by Arpz on Wikimedia
Used under Creative Commons License CC-BY-SA-4.0

Shinty (p26) by Ally Middleton on Flickr
Used under Creative Commons License CC-BY-2.0

Theo Walcott (p26) by Ronnie Macdonald on Flickr
Used under Creative Commons License CC-BY-2.0

Arsene Wenger (p27) by Ronnie Macdonald on Flickr
Used under Creative Commons License CC-BY-2.0

José Mourinho (p27) by Aleksandr Osipov on Flickr
Used under Creative Commons License CC-BY-SA-2.0

Stockings (p27) by Lesley Chandler on Flickr
Used under Creative Commons License CC-BY-2.0

Christopher Biggins (p28) by David Saunders on Flickr
Used under Creative Commons License CC-BY-SA-2.0

Mo Farah (p28) by Citizen59 on Flickr
Used under Creative Commons License CC-BY-SA-2.0

Lewis Hamilton (p28) by Morio on Wikimedia
Used under Creative Commons License CC-BY-SA-4.0

Solihull Sign (p31) by Elliott Brown on Flickr
Used under Creative Commons License CC-BY-2.0

Cottage Pie (p32) by Rudi Riet on Flickr
Used under Creative Commons License CC-BY-SA-2.0

London Zoo Sign (p33) by Matt Brown on Flickr
Used under Creative Commons License CC-BY-2.0

Ricky Martin (p34) by Eva Rinaldi on Flickr
Used under Creative Commons License CC-BY-SA-2.0

High Street (p35) by Beata May on Wikimedia
Used under Creative Commons License CC-BY-SA-3.0

Where's Wally (p35) by William Murphy on Flickr
Used under Creative Commons License CC-BY-SA-2.0

York (Aerial) (p35) by DACP on Geograph
Used under Creative Commons License CC-BY-2.0

Skegness Pier (p35) by MOTORAL 1987 on Wikimedia
Used under Creative Commons License CC-BY-SA-3.0

Drive Thru (p38) by Tony Bernard on Flickr
Used under Creative Commons License CC-BY-SA-2.0

Greensleeves Sheet Music (p39) by Redpaul1 on Wikimedia
Used under Creative Commons License CC-BY-SA-4.0

Chippenham Roundabout (p40) by Rodhullandemu on Wikimedia
Used under Creative Commons License CC-BY-SA-4.0

Witch Doctor (p41) by Joe Mabel on Wikimedia
Used under Creative Commons License CC-BY-SA-3.0

 **Hard Rock Cafe, London** (p41) by Adz2042 on Wikimedia
Used under Creative Commons License CC-BY-SA-4.0

 **Gregg's Counter** (p42) by Rerrj on Wikimedia
Used under Creative Commons License CC-BY-SA-4.0

 **Taser** (p44) by Junglecat on Wikimedia
Used under Creative Commons License CC-BY-SA-3.0

 Chav (p46) by TheArches on Flickr
Used under Creative Commons License CC-BY-2.0

 Yellow Pages (p48) by How can I recycle this on Flickr
Used under Creative Commons License CC-BY-2.0

 **Shopping Trolley in River** (p49) by Albert Bridge on Geograph
Used under Creative Commons License CC-BY-2.0

 **Chingford Post Office** (p50) by Julian Osley on Geograph
Used under Creative Commons License CC-BY-2.0

 Clock (p51) by Paul Downey on Flickr
Used under Creative Commons License CC-BY-2.0

 **Speaking Clock** (p52) by Andrewrabbott on Wikimedia
Used under Creative Commons License CC-BY-SA-4.0

 **Police Stinger** (p53) by West Midlands Police on Flickr
Used under Creative Commons License CC-BY-SA-2.0

 Blancmange (p57) by SKopp on Wikimedia
Used under Creative Commons License CC-BY-SA-3.0

 **Blu Tack** (p64) by Tim Walker on Flickr
Used under Creative Commons License CC-BY-2.0

 **Greenwich Observatory** (p66) by Mike Peel on Wikimedia
Used under Creative Commons License CC-BY-SA-4.0

 Inuit People (p66) by Ansgar Walk on Wikimedia
Used under Creative Commons License CC-BY-SA-3.0

 **Monopoly** (p67) by Chris Potter on Flickr
Used under Creative Commons License CC-BY-2.0

 **Subway** (p72) by Vladis159 on Wikimedia
Used under Creative Commons License CC-BY-SA-4.0

Girl Guides (p73) by Girl Guides of Canada on Flickr
Used under Creative Commons License CC-BY-2.0

 **Chalfont & Latimer Station** (p76) by Sunil060902 on Flickr
Used under Creative Commons License CC-BY-SA-3.0

 **Richard Hammond** (p74) by Howard Lake on Flickr
Used under Creative Commons License CC-BY-SA-2.0

 Miranda Hart (p78) by rodwey2004 on Flickr
Used under Creative Commons License CC-BY-SA-2.0

 Club Biscuit (p83) by Ubcule on Wikimedia
Used under Creative Commons License CC-BY-SA-4.0

 **Timmy Mallett** (p83) by Dave Smith on Flickr
Used under Creative Commons License CC-BY-2.0

 **George Osbourne** (p84) by altogetherfool on Flickr
Used under Creative Commons License CC-BY-SA-2.0

 Piers Morgan (p84) by Nan Palmero on Flickr
Used under Creative Commons License CC-BY-2.0

 Alex Jones (p85) by Daicaregos on Wikimedia
Used under Creative Commons License CC-BY-3.0

 Mel Gibson (p85) by Jeff Turner on Flickr
Used under Creative Commons License CC-BY-2.0

 **Toy Poodle** (p86) by Basile Morin on Wikimedia
Used under Creative Commons License CC-BY-SA-4.0

 Ian Paisley (p86) by MaxM on Wikimedia
Used under Creative Commons License CC-BY-SA-3.0

 **Ambulance** (p86) by Makizox on Wikimedia
Used under Creative Commons License CC-BY-SA-4.0

 **Christopher Nolan** (p87) by Brokensphere on Wikimedia
Used under Creative Commons License CC-BY-SA-3.0

 **Oboe Player** (p89) by Samuraijohnny on Wikimedia
Used under Creative Commons License CC-BY-SA-2.0

 **Village Peopl 1978** (p89) by Mario Casciano on Wikimedia
Used under Creative Commons License CC-BY-SA-3.0

Katy Perry (p89) by slgckgc on Flickr
Used under Creative Commons License CC-BY-2.0

 **Potato Croquettes** (p94) by Marco Verch on Flickr
Used under Creative Commons License CC-BY-2.0

 **Corned Beef Sandwich** (p2) by jeffreyw on Flickr
Used under Creative Commons License CC-BY-2.0

 **Alphabetti Spaghetti** (p97) by Birthe Van Der Veken on Flickr
Used under Creative Commons License CC-BY-2.0

 **Beer Mats** (p97) by Pavel Ševela on Wikimedia
Used under Creative Commons License CC-BY-SA-3.0

 **Welcome Mat** (p97) by The McClouds on Flickr
Used under Creative Commons License CC-BY-SA-2.0

 **Rhubarb Crumble** (p105) by Jasja Dekker on Flickr
Used under Creative Commons License CC-BY-2.0

 Space Raiders (p106) by Havaska on Wikimedia
Used under Creative Commons License CC-BY-SA-3.0

 **Gregg's Shop Front** (p110) by N3ws0fa on Wikimedia
Used under Creative Commons License CC-BY-SA-4.0

 **99 Ice Cream** (p111) by distillated on Flickr
Used under Creative Commons License CC-BY-SA-2.0

 **Markham Moor Little Chef** (p111) by Lobsan on Wikimedia
Used under Creative Commons License CC-BY-SA-3.0

 Kinder Surprise (p114) by Tiia Monto on Wikimedia
Used under Creative Commons License CC-BY-SA-4.0